B in'
with You
This Way

written by **W. Nikola-Lisa**
illustrated by **Michael Bryant**

Lee & Low Books Inc.
New York

Printed in Hong Kong by South China Printing Co. (1988) Ltd.

Book Design by Christy Hale
Book Production by Our House

The text is set in 16 point Folio Medium
The illustrations are rendered in watercolor and colored pencil
10 9 8 7 6 5 4 3
First Edition

Library of Congress Cataloging-in-Publication Data
Nikola-Lisa, W.
Bein' with You This Way / by W. Nikola-Lisa ;
illustrated by Michael Bryant. — First ed.
p.   cm.
ISBN 1-880000-26-1 (paperback)
1. Ethnic groups—Juvenile poetry. 2. Children's poetry, American.
[1. Ethnic groups—Poetry.
2. Brotherliness—Poetry. 3. American poetry.]
I. Bryant, Michael, ill. II. Title.
PS3564.I375B45 1994
811'.54—dc20   93-5164
CIP AC

To the beauty of people,
the wonder of childhood—W.N.L.

For my wife, Gina,
and my children, Kristen and Allison,
whose laughter and giggles help me
remember the joy of childhood—M.B.

Hey, everybody, are you ready?
Uh-huh!
Then snap those fingers
and tap those toes,
and sing along with me.

All right!
Here we go...

She has straight hair.
He has curly hair.
How perfectly
remarkably
strange,
Uh-huh!

Straight hair.
Curly hair.
Different—
Mm-mmm,
but the same,
Ah-ha!

Now isn't it beautiful,
  simply unusual,
  bein' with you
  this way!

Say, what a big nose!
Hey, what a little nose!
How perfectly
  remarkably
  strange,
  Uh-huh!

Big nose.
 Little nose.
Straight hair.
 Curly hair.
Different—
 Mm-mmm,
but the same,
 Ah-ha!

Now isn't it satisfying,
 simply electrifying,
bein' with you
 this way!

Now his eyes are brown.
And her eyes are blue.
How perfectly
remarkably
strange,
Uh-huh!

Brown eyes.
Blue eyes.
Big nose.
Little nose.
Straight hair.
Curly hair.
Different—
Mm-mmm,
but the same,
Ah-ha!

I said isn't it incredible,
  simply unforgettable,
bein' with you
  this way!

Wow, those are thick arms!
Hey, those are thin arms!
How perfectly
  remarkably
    strange,
Uh-huh!

Thick arms.
　Thin arms.
Brown eyes.
　Blue eyes.
Big nose.
　Little nose.
Straight hair.
　Curly hair.
Different—
Mm-mmm,
but the same,
Ah-ha!

Now isn't it fabulous,
　simply enrapturous,
bein' with you
　this way!

Look at those long legs!
Look at those short legs!
How perfectly
remarkably
strange,
Uh-huh!

Long legs.
Short legs.
Thick arms.
Thin arms.
Brown eyes.
Blue eyes.
Big nose.
Little nose.
Straight hair.
Curly hair.
Different—
Mm-mmm,
but the same,
Ah-ha!

Now isn't it terrific,
   simply exquisite,
bein' with you
   this way!

Her skin is light.
His skin is dark.
How perfectly
   remarkably
   strange,
Uh-huh!

Light skin.
Dark skin.
Long legs.
Short legs.
Thick arms.
Thin arms.
Brown eyes.
Blue eyes.
Big nose.
Little nose.
Straight hair.
Curly hair.
Different—
Mm-mmm,
but the same,
Ah-ha!

Now isn't it delightful,
simply out-of-sightful,
bein' with you
this way!

I said, isn't it delightful,
 totally insightful,
 bein' with you
 this way!

Be-bop-a-doo-bop.
 Be-bop-boo.
Be-bop-a-doo-bop.
 Doo-be-dee-doo.

Oh yeah!

Be-bop-a-doo-bop.
Be-bop-boo.
Be-bop-a-doo-bop.
Doo-be-dee-doo.

Mm-mmm!

Be-bop-a-doo-bop.
Be-bop-boo.
Be-bop-a-doo-bop.
Doo-be-dee-doo.

That's right!

And we're gonna be like this
all the rest of our lives,
so come and be with us...

we're on our way!

HEY!